MW00943767

Endorsements

Another 60 Minutes of Wisdom: Growth on the Go is a contemporary book of proverbs. Dr. Derek Grier has distilled years of pragmatic wisdom based in the Scriptures, as well as life experiences, to help us grow on the go. Be ready for "Aha!" and "Wow!" moments as life begins to make sense and you find biblical solutions to chronic issues. Are you ready to grow? You have the growth tool in your hands ... Read and share with others. You can know, grow, and show.

—Dr. Samuel R. Chand
Author of *Cracking Your Church's Culture Code*

The Word of God is powerful. And the Word of God explained by the man of God is priceless. Practical life skills delivered with holy influence leads to powerful living. This is a great read that had me thirsting for more. *Another 60 Minutes of Wisdom: Growth on the Go* will inspire, encourage, and motivate those that read it.

—Marcus D. Wiley
Radio personality and comedian

Derek Grier's words are insightful, motivating and applicable. His brief lessons are easy to read, easy to remember and they will impact your thinking and your life!

—Pastor John K. Jenkins Sr.
First Baptist Church of Glenarden

ANOTHER

60 Minutes of
WISDOM

GROWTH ON THE GO

DEREK GRIER

WestBow
PRESS
A DIVISION OF THOMAS NELSON

WestBow Press books may be ordered through booksellers or by contacting:

WestBow Press
A Division of Thomas Nelson
1663 Liberty Drive
Bloomington, IN 47403
www.westbowpress.com
1-(866) 928-1240

Because of the dynamic nature of the Internet, any web addresses or links contained in
this book may have changed since publication and may no longer be valid. The views
expressed in this work are solely those of the author and do not necessarily reflect the
views of the publisher, and the publisher hereby disclaims any responsibility for them.

ISBN: 978-1-4497-9154-4 (sc)
ISBN: 978-1-4497-9155-1 (e)

Library of Congress Control Number: 2013906961

Printed in the United States of America.
WestBow Press rev. date: 07/29/2013

CONTENTS

Acknowledgments

My darling wife, Yeromitou, you are still my girlfriend. Thank you for being so stress free and such a big part of my world. Boys, you are now young men and being your dad has been the highlight of my life. I am so proud of both of you.

To the Grace Church staff, you are a lot of fun to work with. Your energy is unparalleled. To the Grace Church family, thank you for allowing me to serve so many others outside our congregation. My prayer is that I always represent you well.

Special thanks to Dr. Sam Chand for being a sounding board and offering invaluable advice throughout the years. John Maxwell and John Hull, serving through EQUIP has been a joy.

Foreword

What will take more work: preparing to make a one-hour presentation or speaking for one minute with succinct clarity?

No doubt, it will be much more work and rework to distill the essence of a topic into a very small time slot. That's exactly what Dr. Derek Grier has done in *Another 60 Minutes of Wisdom: Growth on the Go.* He has squeezed the nectar and then turned it into concentrate so that in less than a minute, you can grow on the go.

You will notice "RDA" (Required Daily Allowance) on many nutritional labels. That means that you can measure your required daily allowance for ongoing growth and health. *Another 60 Minutes of Wisdom: Growth on the Go* contains your required daily allowance.

I would recommend one spoonful or page per day. It will enhance your internal vim, vigor, and vitality to the degree that others will notice your growth. At that time, with a smile, you can tell them about *Another 60 Minutes of Wisdom: Growth on the Go.*

Dr. Grier is a leader of leaders and does so from a core of integrity, overcoming adversity, and a true desire to help others grow.

You hold your own personal growth plan in your hands. Go ahead. Take a spoonful!

—Sam Chand

Introduction

If you were a pastor and had only sixty seconds to speak to hundreds of thousands of people, in one of the most diverse metropolitan areas in the United States, what would you say? I have wrestled with this question week after week for the last four years.

The pages ahead are a compilation of my sixty-second radio talks that have aired since 2008 in the Washington, DC, metropolitan area. *60 Minutes of Wisdom: Insight in an Instant*, released in 2009, was the first book in this series. Since the publishing of that book, we have received many requests for written copies of the newer radio *Ministry Minutes*, and this book is the result.

Take this journey with me, and in sixty minutes, you will experience personal growth, be able to build stronger relationships, and become a better leader. Not only will you become wiser and sharper, but most importantly, you will begin to see God in a fresh way.

PERSONAL GROWTH

"All things being equal, it is the healthy tree that will be the most productive. If we focus on becoming healthy, fruitfulness will soon follow."

–DEREK GRIER

MINUTE 61

Discovering God's Will for Your Life

First Thessalonians 5:16–18 says, "Rejoice always, pray continually, give thanks in all circumstances; for this is God's will for you." If you are wondering what God's will is for your life, question no more.

God's will is that we rejoice, pray, and be thankful, no matter our circumstances. You might say, "How could God ask for so much from us?" I say, "Why did He ask us for so little?" Even if we don't have a lot to be thankful for in life, we can be thankful for this: When we are good, God loves us. When we are bad, He loves us. When we are confused, He loves us. When we are sad, He loves us.

If you did not think you had anything to be thankful for a few minutes ago, you should now. Discovering God's will for our lives begins with an attitude, not an assignment. Take a few minutes to personally experience God's will by being grateful.

MINUTE 62

Imitation

To be a disciple of Christ is a powerful thing. Discipleship not only implies submission but also imitation. Jesus said in Matthew 10:25, "It is enough for students to be *like* their teachers, and servants *like* their masters." Genuine discipleship causes imitation.

No matter how loudly you sing or how often you attend church on Sunday, if you act like the Devil the rest of the week, you are not a disciple of Christ. Genuine disciples have bad days, make bad choices, and even sin at times, but this is the exception and not the rule.

We miss the mark for one of three reasons.

1. We try to live up to the wrong standards. (We follow human ideas instead of God's Word.)
2. We have the wrong source of strength. (We try to do it by sheer willpower instead of reliance on the Holy Spirit.)
3. We have the wrong motives. (We are trying to please people and not God.)

To love Jesus is to ask Him to help you be like Him.

MINUTE 63

Stop Coping

I heard someone say today that COPE stands for Covering, Over, Pain, Effectively. In church, people can become masters at coping, experts at masking the pain in their hearts. We learn to get our praise *on* and lift our hands *up*. We give the person sitting *beside* us a high five, and after church, we know how to go to our favorite restaurants and *get down*. But Jesus did not die for us to create a new *coping* mechanism. He rose to give us a new *hoping* mechanism.

When is the last time you really told the Lord what was going on in your heart? David said in Psalm 18:6 (ESV), "In my distress I called upon the Lord." David did not pretend that he was okay when he was not. He said, "To my God I cried for help. From his temple he heard my voice, and my cry to him reached his ears." God will be more real to you, when you get real with Him. Do more than *cope*. Begin to put your *hope* in God.

MINUTE 64

How Far We Have Come

Ephesians 4:15 says, "Speaking the truth in love, we will grow." Did you know that God does not require us to be perfect, but He does expect us to grow? Paul finished the verse by saying, "to become in every respect the mature body." God wants us not only to grow but also to mature.

When my kids were in diapers, I did not enjoy changing them, but I never got mad at them for making it so I had to. My kids did what healthy children did at that stage of life.

God has often had to clean up after me. Instead of being angry, God understood that it was just a stage of life, and I would soon get past it. God is not requiring that any of us come to Him behaving perfectly, but He does desire that we improve. The real measurement of progress is not how perfect we are, but how far we have come.

MINUTE 65

Extraordinary

I heard someone say that only five letters stand between ordinary and extraordinary: e–x–t–r–a. Investing just a little extra effort, a little extra focus, and just a little extra time can make a remarkable difference in your life.

Song of Solomon 2:15 states it is the little foxes that ruin the vine. Often it's not the big things that get in the way of progress but the little things.

When I wanted to lose weight, cutting out sodas for a month and drinking a little extra water helped me lose pounds. When our budget became tight, a little more staying-in versus going-out saved us hundreds of dollars each month. Our family started to get a little disconnected, so we simply decided to turn off the TV while eating dinner. A little extra conversation turned our house back into a home. It only takes a little *extra* to start living an extraordinary life.

MINUTE 66

Handling Responsibility

The early church not only experienced explosive growth but also explosive problems. In Acts 6:3, the apostles came up with the solution. "Brothers and sisters, choose seven men from among you who are known to be full of the Spirit and wisdom. We will turn this responsibility over to them." There are dozens of leadership principles in this one verse, but during a very challenging period, the one word that jumped off the page was *responsibility*.

The word can be broken into two parts: *response* and *ability*. It became clear that if God gave me responsibility, it is because He has placed in me the ability to respond appropriately to the given demands. Accepting responsibility does not mean that we must do everything ourselves. The way the disciples handled their growing responsibilities was to give them away. The best leaders do not measure themselves by what they can do themselves but by what they can do through others.

MINUTE 67

Giving

Ralph Waldo Emerson observed, "One of the most beautiful compensations of this life is that we cannot sincerely try to help others without helping ourselves."[1] In Luke 6:38, Jesus put it this way, "Give, and it will be given to you."

The very act of giving frees us from the wearisomeness of only having ourselves on our minds. Giving always does more for the giver than the receiver. Giving is the highest expression of God's image in us. Generosity is not an obligation but a privilege. Look for an opportunity to help you by helping someone else today. Remember to do it with no strings attached if you want to experience the greatest benefits of giving.

MINUTE 68

Know When to Run

There is an old country song that I found to be very instructive when dealing with temptation. "You got to know when to hold 'em, know when to fold 'em. Know when to walk away, know when to run."[2]

Genesis 39:6–12 says,

> Now Joseph was well-built and handsome, and after a while his master's wife took notice of Joseph and said, "Come to bed with me!" But he refused … Then, one day, Joseph went into the house to attend to his duties, and none of the household servants were inside. She caught him by his cloak and said, "Come to bed with me!" But he left his cloak in her hand and ran out of the house.

Joseph did more than attempt to resist; he knew when it was time to run. When your personal resistance fails, don't be above putting on your running shoes. Learning when to resist, and when to leave the room, may determine whose bed you wind up in tonight.

MINUTE 69

Hold Your Horses

Abraham was the first to call God "Jehovah Jireh," which some say literally means, "the One who sees ahead and provides." Whatever God calls for, He will first provide for.

Imagine if Adam grew impatient and could have convinced God to create him on the first day. Since the ground was not made until the third day, Adam would have had to swim forty-eight hours before he could stand. If Adam had to wait his turn, then so do you.

Ecclesiastes 3:11 says, "He has made everything beautiful in its time." Like the movement in a well-oiled engine, keeping pace with God is a beautiful thing.

When we lag behind or get ahead of God's timing, what was intended for glory becomes another story. What He intended to bless can quickly turn into a mess. The problem is never God's unfaithfulness, but sometimes our impatience. Hold your horses, and you will one day hold your blessings.

MINUTE 70

A Joyful Heart

Proverbs 17:22 says, "A joyful heart is good medicine." (ESV) Before modern science acknowledged the interconnectedness between our bodies and souls, the writer of Proverbs was inspired to observe that cheerfulness does a body good. Our disposition of mind has a profound impact upon the condition of our bodies. Proverbs continues, "But a crushed spirit dries up the bones." A sorrowful heart not only weakens our nerves but also impacts our very bones. The writer is teaching us that no emotion has a greater capacity for destruction than unresolved bitterness and grief.

Sometimes, we should look deeper at our physical symptoms; they may be trying to point at more profound issues. If we learn to lighten up and brighten up, we may all make fewer trips to the doctor. Life is too short to live it sad.

MINUTE 71

Back in the Driver's Seat

One thing I love about Jesus is how deliberate He is. When speaking of his impending death, He flipped the script and said, "No man takes my life but I lay it down." When Peter took issue with Him saying He would die on the cross, Jesus refused to let a human relationship get in the way of his relationship with His heavenly father, and He sternly rebuked the senior disciple. Then Jesus made this telling statement in John 15:16 to all his disciples: "You did not choose me, but I chose you." Jesus made choices about who was in His life and did not leave such decisions to circumstances or others.

Life is too short to let other people live it for you. It is important that you start sitting in the driver's seat of your life. You cannot change your past, but you can change your future. Start by making prayerful choices about who is in it.

MINUTE 72
A Stick for Backs of Fools

Proverbs 26:3 says, "A whip for the horse, a halter for the donkey, and a rod for the back of fools!" Why is a stick destined for the backs of fools? Because if we are not responsive when God speaks to us through His Word and as the voice of our consciences, God has to speak to us through the only language a fool understands: pain.

We often hurt in our lives, not because God does not love us but because we would not listen any other way. When my children were little, I would say, "If you do not listen to my mouth, you will have to feel my hand." This is frowned upon today, but it worked well for my kids. They became fast learners.

If we have a soft heart before God, He can deal with us gently. But if our hearts are hard, we force God to be hard. Sometimes our lives are hard because our heads are so hard.

MINUTE 73
Tips for Confrontation

Confrontation contains the prefix *con*, which means "together," and the root *fron*, which means "face." It speaks of the act of coming together face-to-face to resolve an issue. Confrontation is a normal part of life and a skill that you must master if you want to be successful.

Two questions may help you in this area. Before your next confrontation, ask yourself, "Should I confront this person or let it go?" Proverbs 19:11 says, "It is to one's glory to overlook an offense." In other words, do not be petty. Be big enough to let the minor slights and digs pass, and only confront when you need to.

Secondly, ask yourself if your attitude is right. A confrontation with a friend should never be about retaliation. Avoid attacking the person's motivations and character. Only God knows what is really going on in a person's heart. Focus only on the behavior and the impact that the person's behavior has on him or her and you in particular. An old saying will help you maintain your boundaries in the midst of conflict: "Keep your words sweet, because you may have to eat them."

MINUTE 74

Making the Most of My Time

Today, I want to borrow some insights from John Maxwell. He stated, "We cannot manage time. We can only manage opportunities."[3] We cannot change how much time we are given, but we can take advantage of each day's opportunities. Time is life's most precious commodity. He goes on to say, "We cannot change time, only our priorities."[4] Everyone gets twenty-four hours in a day, but how we use our time is what makes the difference.

Wise people do not spend time but invest it. What we value in life is seen clearest by how we make use of our time. Why do we spend so much time watching other people live on television, instead of living ourselves? We can always catch the rerun. Why do we spend so much time trying to impress people we do not really know and, if we are honest, do not even like? The people that are so important to us today we will probably not even see five years from now. People, places, and things will change, but we will never get any more time. So invest it in things that matter.

MINUTE 75

No More Monkey Business

I have heard that in Australia there is a special method for catching monkeys. People put a piece of fruit in a little box with a hole big enough for the monkey to stick his open hand through. The hunters then leave the boxes under a tree overnight and return in the morning to find the monkeys with their hands caught and unable to get free.

All the monkeys had to do to get out of the trap was to open their hands. But once the monkey had the piece of fruit in hand, he refused to let go of it. The box would release an open hand but not a fist.

Our inability to let go of the things that are in our possession is often the reason why we are trapped.

MINUTE 76

Breaking Habits

A habit is anything we do repetitively without consciously thinking about it. The brain is a sophisticated and efficient machine, and it does not waste its time starting from scratch every time a decision needs to be made. Our brains take what we have done in the past as our recommendation of what we want to do in the future.

If our past decisions were good, this pre-wiring will serve us well. But if our past decisions were poor, we can become trapped by our past behavior.

Romans 12:2 says, "Do not conform to the pattern of this world, but be transformed by the renewing of your mind." The best way to overcome an old behavior is by creating a new one. Give your mind better recommendations to choose from. Your mind was designed to be influenced by your behavior. Your old habits begin with a choice, and new ones can begin with a choice. I am not promising that it will be easy; I am saying that the choice is yours.

MINUTE 77

Renewed Reasoning

Hebrews 11:17-19 says, "By faith Abraham, when God tested him, offered Isaac as a sacrifice, even though God had said to him, 'It is through Isaac that your offspring will be reckoned.' Listen to the next verse. "Abraham reasoned that God could even raise the dead." Don't miss this. Abraham did not have a specific word that his son would come back to life; he simply surmised it.

Some of us are waiting on a word from God to calm our fears. But when we begin to reason properly, many of our apprehensions will go away by themselves. "Abraham *reasoned* that God could even raise the dead" (emphasis added). How do you think when you are in crisis? Do you reason like Father Abraham? "If God led me here, He must have a plan to get me out." Or "If this difficult thing happened, I must have the wherewithal to handle it, because God promised that we would not be tempted beyond what we can bear."

We will not need so many miracles of supernatural comfort if we start thinking right. Use your head.

MINUTE 78

Trust

Scripture teaches us to love unconditionally but never tells us to trust unconditionally. Jesus says in Luke 16:10, "Whoever can be trusted with very little can also be trusted with much, and whoever is dishonest with very little will also be dishonest with much." The principle is that before we trust people with big things, we need to give them a chance to prove themselves with small things.

Proverbs 11:22 says, "Like a gold ring in a pig's snout is a beautiful woman who shows no discretion." Discretion is the restraint people who realize their significance must use, to protect their lives from abuse. If we make our most valued treasures free for the asking, Scripture says it is like putting a five-karat nose ring in the snout of a pig. The pig does not know the ring's value and will only take what is precious to you back into its mire.

Let people earn your trust, so you can spend less time having to recover your treasures from the mud.

MINUTE 79

Much Fruit

Jesus says in John 15:8 (ESV), "By this My Father is glorified, that you bear much fruit." How long would an owner of an orchard keep trees that were just hanging on, barely surviving and not producing fruit? Not long. The owner would eventually cut those trees down and plant new ones. The trees were not planted just to exist; they were planted to produce.

Jesus said, "By this my Father is glorified, that you bear much fruit and so prove to be my disciples." As the orchard owner does not plant trees just to take up space but to produce, so does our heavenly Father create us with an expectation of fruitfulness. The proof of our discipleship is not only our church attendance or the songs we sing but also the lives we live. God has not designed us just to be present; He has created us to thrive.

MINUTE 80

Making a Consequence

We are free to choose, but we will never be free from the consequences of our choices. God said to Adam and Eve in Genesis 2:17, "You must not eat from the tree of the knowledge of good and evil, for when you eat of it you will certainly die." God gave Adam and Eve the liberty to choose or reject Him at the tree, but He also made clear that they would have to live with the consequences of their choice.

Making a decision is not hard; it is living with the consequences of our decisions that can be tough. Keep in mind that every time you make a decision, your decision is also making a consequence.

MINUTE 81

The First Step

When I was a kid, I used to sit in my friend's old car and pretend to drive. When the car was parked and the ignition was off, it was almost impossible to turn the wheel. Typically, we cannot change the direction of a car unless it is moving. Likewise, God cannot steer the lives of people who insist on sitting still.

You might say, "When God gives me a complete plan, then I will move." But Psalm 37:23 (KJV) says, "The *steps* of a good man are ordered by the LORD" (emphasis added). If you are not willing to take your first step, you will not hear God's next step. God often shows us His plan, one step at a time. A little motion will turn your life around.

MINUTE 82

What We Believe about Ourselves

Carter G. Woodson said,

> If you can control a man's thinking, you don't have to worry about his actions. If you can determine what a man thinks you don't have to worry about what he will do. If you can make a man feel he is inferior, you don't have to compel him to seek inferior status, he will do so without being told and if you can make a man believe that he is justly an outcast, you don't have to order him to the backdoor, he will go to the backdoor on his own and if there is no backdoor, the very nature of the man will demand that he build one.[5]

We will always act in a manner consistent with what we believe about ourselves. Proverbs 23:7 (KJV) says, "As a man thinks in his heart so is he." Change your mind, and you will change your life.

MINUTE 83

When Will My Man Be Ready?

Marriage is not for everyone. Jesus was single. Paul, Daniel, John the Baptist, and many others lived powerful lives without being married. But for those women who want to marry, how do you know when a man is ready for marriage?

Three things were present in Adam before God brought Eve.

1. The man had a job. Genesis 2:15 says, "The LORD God took the man and put him in the Garden of Eden to work it and take care of it." Ladies, your attitude should be, "No money, no honey."

2. Adam knew God's voice. Verse 16 says, "And the Lord God commanded the man, 'You are free to eat from any tree in the garden.'" Ladies, your attitude should be, "Don't know God, won't know me."

3. Adam had clear boundaries in his life. In verse 17, the Lord said to Adam, "You must not eat from the tree of the knowledge of good and evil, for when you eat from it you will certainly die." Ladies, if a man can't tell himself "no," you'd better.

Another 60 Minutes of Wisdom

MINUTE 84

How to Overcome Temper

Both of my parents are African American, but my middle name is McCurry because my great, great grandfather was Irish. I can easily fit both stereotypes of the angry Black man and the Irish temper. On top of this, my father's father was a full-blooded Native American, so I could watch *Amistad, Braveheart,* and *Dances with Wolves* and walk out my house with a shotgun.

Kidding aside, I really do understand temper. The thing that helped me manage my temper was first understanding that anger is not bad in itself. Even Jesus got angry and turned over tables. Ephesians 4:26 does not say, "In your anger, you sin," but "In your anger, *do* not sin."

When righteousness is violated, it is healthy to feel angry. But how we handle this emotion is key. When I feel angry, I have learned to focus on the principle and not the people, to attack the problem and not the person. I am not always as successful at this as I would like, but I am getting better.

28

MINUTE 85

How Not to Handle Mistakes

I wanted to title this *Ministry Minute* "How to Handle Mistakes." Then I thought about the many mistakes I have made and decided we should first focus on how not to handle a mistake.

There are three things we should not to do when we make a mistake.

1. Don't try to cover it up.
2. Don't try to cover it up.
3. Don't try to cover it up.

In politics, people say the cover-up is always worse than the crime. Our instinct for self-preservation can get us into a lot of trouble. When David tried to cover up his sin with Bathsheba, sex evolved into deception and then into murder. David could have recovered from his initial sin, but he never recovered from the attempted cover-up.

Here are three steps that can help you when you miss:

1. Admit your mistake quickly. Don't delay the inevitable.

2. Accept responsibility. The Devil did not make you do it, though he probably helped you out. You did it.

3. Ask for help from someone in authority. Authority should not be run from but run to, when we are in trouble.

Section 2

RELATIONSHIPS

"Jesus said, 'Treat others the same way you want to be treated.' If you want to become somebody, you must first realize that there are no nobodies."

— DEREK GRIER

MINUTE 86

Self-Respect

Are things in life happening to you or are you making your life happen? In Deuteronomy 28:13, Moses said, "The Lord will make you the head and not the tail." What is the difference between being a head and a tail? First, the view is much better. But secondly, the head makes decisions that the tail is obligated to follow.

I remember the day I got tired of feeling like a victim. People were pushing, pulling, and grabbing at me to make me what they wanted me to be, until I recognized that it is impossible to please everyone.

I realized that no matter what I did, I would face criticism and certain people would find fault with me. I decided that, if I was going to be talked about anyway, I might as well be talked about for being myself. I decided I would no longer suffer for trying to be the person I could never be, but I should be willing to take the heat for the person I am. It's amazing how people will respect a person who decides to respect themselves.

MINUTE 87

Saying "No" without Explanation

When Nehemiah's enemies discovered that he had rebuilt the wall and not a gap was left in it, they sent him this message: "Come, let us meet together in one of the villages on the plain of Ono." (Nehemiah 6:3–4) But Nehemiah discerned that it was a trap. So he replied, "I am carrying on a great project and cannot go down. Four times they sent me the same message, and each time I gave them the same answer."

I can think of dozens of times that I knew in my gut that I was being set up, but in my attempt to be nice, I took the meeting anyway. I have regretted it every time. Scripture says God is love, but it also teaches us that God is wise. I have learned that I do not have to answer every call or accept every invitation. Scripture teaches that we are to owe no man anything but love. An older man once said to me, "A sign of maturity is sometimes being able to say 'no' without explanation."

MINUTE 88

How We Stayed Married

I was at a conference recently and said to myself, "If I hear another 'ought to' message without the speaker explaining to me 'how to,' my head is going to explode. We all know we ought to be better; the question is 'How?'"

Young men often ask me, "How have you remained faithful to your wife for eighteen years?" Based on today's headlines, it is certainly not because I am a preacher. My wife and I have had our challenges, but marriage for us was not just about getting our respective needs met. We took seriously the biblical admonition, "Take up your cross and follow me." (Matthew 16:24, ESV) Sometimes, I was her beam, and sometimes, she was mine.

My goal as a husband is not to have someone who loves me, though my wife does more than I deserve. My goal is to find ways to love my wife. When our primary goal was to give love and not get love, our relationship fell in line. Marriage is probably one of the greatest opportunities in life to help people get over themselves.

MINUTE 89

Love God, Love People

Romans 12:20–21 says, "If your enemy is hungry, feed him; if he is thirsty, give him something to drink. In doing this, you will heap burning coals on his head. Do not be overcome by evil, but overcome evil with good."

If you want to have an effective walk with God, you must keep in mind that God cares about our enemies as much as He cares for us. We often have great excuses for why we have soured in our walk with God, but it usually can be narrowed down to one thing: love. At some point, we stop forgiving people. We have to remember that our bitterness says more about us than those who have done us wrong.

MINUTE 90

Crazy People

Galatians 3:2–6 from The Message Bible says,

> Let me put this question to you: How did your new life begin? Was it by working your heads off to please God? Or was it by responding to God's Message to you? … Only crazy people would think they could complete by their own efforts what was begun by God. If you weren't smart enough or strong enough to begin it, how do you suppose you could perfect it? … Answer this question: Does the God who lavishly provides you with his own presence, his Holy Spirit, working things in your lives you could never do for yourselves, does he do these things because of your strenuous moral striving or because you trust him to do them in you? Don't these things happen among you just as they happened with Abraham? He believed God, and that act of belief was turned into a life that was right with God.

Paul is saying that when we learn to trust God, we no longer have to try so hard.

MINUTE 91

Coming Out of Your Shell

Because of my public life, people are surprised to find that I am not naturally an extrovert but an introvert. I have spent most of my early life somewhat withdrawn. I still do not enjoy being the center of attention, but there is a night-and-day difference between my disposition a few years ago and my attitude today. What happened? What helped me grow?

I discovered at the core of every insecurity is typically selfishness or ignorance. Selfishness, because people cannot be insecure without having themselves on their minds; ignorance, because Psalm 139:14 removes the foundation for all personal insecurity by declaring, "I am fearfully and wonderfully made." *Fearfully* literally means "awe-inspiring." *Wonderfully* communicates the idea of being in a class by oneself. According to Scripture, I am awesome and in a class by myself.

If I believed what this psalm said about me, it would be selfish of me to keep me only to myself. The first step to coming out of a shell is realizing that you are valuable and have something of value to offer to others.

MINUTE 92

Check the Garbage at the Door

Any good team requires both strong coaching and honest communication. When Jesus built his team, He created a culture of openness and honesty within the team. Matthew 16:22–23 is one such example.

Jesus had been talking about his impending death and "Peter took Jesus aside and began to rebuke him. Saying, 'Never, Lord! This shall never happen to you.'" On a good team, the team members are free to speak their minds. But watch this: Jesus turned to Peter and said, "Get behind me, Satan. You are a stumbling block to me. You do not have the concerns of God but merely human concerns."

On a healthy team, not only can the players speak frankly, but so can the coach. I invite my staff to be open and honest with me, but under one condition—I can be equally frank. I have no problem with people telling me about myself, as long as they recognize it is a two-way street and they are comfortable with me doing the same.

MINUTE 93

You Get What You Choose

In Joshua 24:15, God said, "Choose for yourselves today whom you will serve." We do not get what we want in life; we get what we choose. We cannot control everything that happens to us, but we can control our responses.

God can do anything, but one thing He will not do is choose for us. As much as He loves us, He will not make our choices. The best marital advice I ever gave is this: Your central concern in your marriage is not how your spouse treats you, but how you treat your spouse. God does not measure us based on how others treat us but on how we treat others.

MINUTE 94

Ask for Help

Mark 15:20–21 says, "And when they had mocked him … Then they led him out to crucify him." It was customary for the condemned to carry their own cross, but after the events of the last fifteen hours:

- the agonies of Gethsemane, including sweating drops of blood;
- the betrayal of Judas;
- the desertion of His own disciples;
- the denial of His leading disciple, Peter;
- the bloody beating with a Roman nine-prong whip; and
- the crown of thorns and several beatings by the soldiers.

Tradition says Jesus fell under the weight of the cross. The most powerful man who had ever lived became too weak to carry His own load. The Bible says a man from Cyrene was passing by and the soldiers forced him to carry the cross. If Jesus stumbled under the weight of his cross, don't be surprised if you do too. Just be humble enough to accept help.

MINUTE 95
Strong Marriage

I know you have heard me say this before, but I am going to keep saying this until it registers. After years of mentoring couples, I think that the best marriage counseling that could be offered to a starry-eyed couple is to hand them three nails, a hammer, and a cross and tell them they are going to need it.

We have no idea how self-centered we are until we choose to live and make decisions with another person in sickness and health, till death do we part. Marriage is God's sense of humor, having a head on collision with our self-absorption.

Galatians 5:24 says, "Those who belong to Christ Jesus have crucified the flesh with its passions and desires." It did not say that those who go to church have crucified the flesh but those who "belong to Christ." It requires more than attending church to stay in relationships; it takes holiness. Holiness has nothing to do with alcohol, tobacco, or the length of your dress. True holiness is about the holes in your hands and feet. Two truly *hole-y* people will stay together.

MINUTE 96

Star

Proverbs 11:14 says, "For lack of guidance a nation falls, but victory is won through many advisers." Since victory is won through many advisers, our success is not dependent on only what we know but who we listen to.

I have learned to use the STAR acronym to qualify my advisors.

- "S" – Is the person **successful** in the area they offer advice? It is one thing to have an opinion, but it is far better to have a track record.
- "T" – Will the person be **transparent** with me? I need to hear not only about successes but also failures, to truly learn what to avoid.
- "A" – I don't have to always **agree** with the person. If I agree with everything that is said, I am probably not learning anything new.
- "R" – I must **respect** the person. Respect is the currency of all true relationships.

If you soar with the stars, you will shine like one.

MINUTE 97

Choose Your Friends Wisely

In Mark 2:1–5, because a crowd had filled the house to hear Jesus, a paralyzed man could not get inside to meet Him. So his friends dug through the roof and lowered the paralyzed man on a mat. The Bible says Jesus saw their faith and healed him.

If the paralyzed man's friends were like many of our friends, they would have tried to talk him out of trying to get to Jesus. After all, Jesus was an important person, the house was too small, the crowd was too large, and the list goes on. But instead of discouraging the man, they carried him. Sometimes, we can't get by without a little help from our friends. The people we make our friends can make the difference between living outside the place of blessing and going through the roof.

MINUTE 98

A Few

One night, I was considering the state of our world and I cried out to the Lord, "Where is your honor? Where is your respect?" Where is the fear of God in our nation?" After a few moments of silence, the Lord responded, "Where is your faith?"

In Genesis 18:23–26, Abraham argued with the Lord, "Will you sweep away the righteous with the wicked? What if there are fifty righteous people in the city. Will you really sweep it away and not spare the place for the sake of the fifty righteous people in it?" The Lord responded, "If I find fifty righteous people in the city of Sodom, I will spare the whole place for their sake." Then Abraham negotiated down to ten. God promised that He would spare the city for the sake of only ten righteous.

God intervening in our world is not dependent on the wickedness of the wicked but on the righteousness of the righteous.

MINUTE 99

Worth It

I have built several churches in my life. One of the biggest challenges in a construction project is trying to fit the church's growing needs into an attainable budget. Purchase the land, design the project, develop the land, and with what is left, build the building. Often, a church has to cut corners and sacrifice needs to accommodate the bottom line of the financial plan.

The Bible states that we are "God's building." In Luke 14:28, Jesus adds, "Suppose one of you wants to build a tower. Won't you first sit down and estimate the cost to see if you have enough money to complete it?" Don't you think God takes His own advice? Before you were born, God considered exactly what it would cost to build you into the person He wanted you to be. He counted the astronomical cost, spread his arms out wide on a splintered cross, and said, "You are worth it." Without cutting out a space or shrinking His plan, Jesus has provided for our every need, and still has riches to spare.

Oh, how unsearchable, inexhaustible, and thoroughly exceptional is God's plan for each of us.

MINUTE 100

Grow Grass

People who have been in church a long time are often taken back by my philosophy of ministry. Sunday visitors often hand me their resumes and books, looking to obtain a quick platform for their business or ministry. But I have pastored long enough to understand that before I get impressed by your title, I need to see you wearing a towel.

John 13:4 says Jesus got up from the last supper, took off his outer clothing, and wrapped a towel around his waist and began to wash his disciples' feet. To truly lead, one must first learn to serve.

As a servant leader, my ambition is not so much to build a ministry but to build and serve people. When people are strong, the organization is strong. The focus is never on getting more sheep but on growing healthy grass, maintaining a safe environment, and keeping an open door. When a church's leaders have healthy attitudes, you will find a healthy and growing congregation.

MINUTE 101

Organized Religion

I often hear people say, "I am against organized religion." I often want to ask, "Are you saying you are for disorganized religion? Are you for chaos? Organization is a fundamental principle of success."

Ecclesiastes 4:9–10 says two are better than one, because they have a good return for their work. Certain outcomes can only be arrived at through cooperation. This is why darkness tries so desperately to keep us apart.

Ecclesiastes continues. "If one falls down, his friend can help him up." We need each other. Then it says, "But pity the man who falls and has no one to help him up." Certain help will not be available in our lives unless we have strong relationships.

It is vital that each of us discovers the power of maintaining healthy connections with other people. If you can walk alone, it is probably because you are not going very far.

MINUTE 102

Moving

I have been with many people during the last moments of their lives. I remember one dear lady in particular. She said she was not welcome in other churches and came to our services as a last resort. She eventually responded to the message of salvation and was marvelously born again.

She was suffering from AIDS but so hungry for the Sunday teaching that she would inject her feet with needles to numb the pain so that she could come to church. Eventually, her disease ran its course and she was moved into a hospice center.

She did not want to go into the program, but she eventually went in almost kicking and screaming. After she got there, she looked at me with such joy shining in her face that it scared me. She said, "Pastor, I want to go home." I thought she meant back to her apartment. I told her that she could not. She looked at me, reprimanding me with her eyes, as if I of all people should have understood what she meant.

Second Corinthians 5:8 (ESV) declares to be away from the body is to be at home with the Lord. She was no longer resistant, and she was willing to move for the last time.

MINUTE 103

How Could a Loving God Send People to Hell?

People often ask with incredulity, "How could a loving God send people to hell?" I think the more appropriate question is this: "How could anyone be so evil that they would reject the grace of our loving God?" Jesus said in Mathew 25:41, "The king will say to those on his left, 'Depart from me, you who are cursed, into the eternal fire prepared for the devil and his angels.'"

We need to consider two things about hell: First, it was not prepared for people but the Devil. Those of us who go to hell are uninvited guests. We force ourselves in by pushing past God's grace and mercy and insisting on our own way.

Secondly, if all people do, day and night, in heaven is celebrate God's goodness and you can't stand ninety minutes in church, how are you going to handle an eternity of praise? Unless your heart is changed, heaven would be like hell to you. God does not arbitrarily send people to hell. We send ourselves by our unwillingness to embrace His truth and love.

MINUTE 104

Loyalty

In Job 2:2–4, the Lord said to Satan, "Have you considered my servant Job?" … "Skin for skin!" Satan replied. "A man will give all he has for his own life … Strike his flesh and bones, and he will surely curse you to your face."

Satan is a cynic. He was implying that Job obeyed God only because of what God *did* for him, not because of what God *meant* to him. Trials don't come because God does not care for us but because the Devil is cynical about our faith.

I remember a time in my life when doctors could not cure my disease. I was in debt, my board was talking of firing me, and friends and family were far and few between. It seemed like everything I touched fell apart. I put on a front during the day, but when my wife and kids were asleep, I would go into my closet, kneel on the floor, and worship with quiet tears.

I did not understand all that was happening in my life, but I could not abandon the One who would never abandon me. I would say with Job, "Though he slay me, yet will I trust in him." (Job 13:15, NKJV) Sometimes faith is spelled l–o–y–a–l–t–y.

MINUTE 105

Jesus Loves Me

Paul says in Romans 8:38-39,

> For I am convinced that neither death nor life, neither angels nor demons, neither the present nor the future, nor any powers, neither height nor depth, nor anything else in all creation, will be able to separate us from the love of God that is in Christ Jesus our Lord.

What does God want us to be convinced of? Convinced that we are always right? That certain things will go as planned? No. Paul changed the world because he was convinced of one thing: that God loved him. Are you fully persuaded, certain, and knowing beyond a shadow of a doubt that sickness or health, life or death, the angelic or demonic, time or space, or thinkable or unthinkable cannot get between you and God's love for you? Our theology has become too adult when we forget the simple lyrics we learned as a child. "Jesus loves me, this I know, for the Bible tells me so." Jesus said, "Truly, I say to you, whoever does not receive the kingdom of God like a child shall not enter it." (Luke 18:17, ESV)

MINUTE 106

The Lottery

A mathematician made an observation that stuck with me. "God is so big that all of eternity fits on his insides." We tend to see the past, present, and future in a linear fashion, but God stands outside of time and looks at the past, present, and future all at once.

In Isaiah 46:9–10 (NKJV), God says, "I am God, and there is no other… I make known the end from the beginning, from ancient times, what is still to come…" Years ago, two scientists calculated the probability that just eight predictions of the Messiah would be fulfilled in one person: place of birth, type of death, gender, mother, ethnicity, etc. He came up with odds of one in one hundred quadrillion. Astronomical! Mathematically speaking, it is over one million times more likely to win the lottery than for Jesus not to be the Messiah. You will have far better odds investing your dollar at church next Sunday than buying your next lottery ticket.

MINUTE 107

Making Time to Pray

I happen to serve at a very large church with a lot of needs. I lead four services each Sunday and have meetings in-between. I teach another three to five times a week, conduct funerals, weddings, and hospital visitations, serve families in crisis, counsel, address media, oversee our administrative and organizational needs, and the list goes on. I don't get more hours in a day because I am called to the ministry. I only get twenty-four hours like everybody else.

Charles Spurgeon once said, "I have so much to do to-day that I shall never get through it with less than three hours' prayer."[6] I am learning the more I have to do, the more I need to make time for God. For every hour I invest in prayer, I am saved double by not having to do the extra work of fixing things I would otherwise break.

You think you don't have time to pray, but the truth is you don't have enough time not to pray.

MINUTE 108

Punished for Our Peace

Would you worship a loving God even though He was unjust? You might appease Him but could never truly respect such a God. There is only one place in history where God's absolute love and justice collide. Isaiah 53:5 says of Jesus, "But he was pierced for our transgressions, he was crushed for our iniquities; the punishment that brought us peace was on him."

Justice required that sin be punished, but mercy desired to spare the guilty. This reminds me of a story about a judge in a small town. His son was caught speeding and had to appear before his father in court. It was a test, but the father had to find his son guilty. After the hearing, he took off his black robe and reached into his own pocket and paid his son's fine.

The cross was God reaching into His own pocket to pay the penalty for our sins. The punishment that brought us peace was paid by Him. What happened on Calvary was the most profound example of integrity, wisdom, and mercy ever!

MINUTE 109

Wounded so We Could Be Healed

Few people question whether God forgives, but many debate whether Jesus still heals. In the first century, the debate was reversed. People believed that God healed but questioned whether Jesus had the authority to forgive.

In Luke 5:20–24, some men brought a sick man to Jesus who stated, "Your sins are forgiven." The Pharisees began thinking, "Who is this fellow who speaks blasphemy? Who can forgive sins but God alone?"

Listen to Christ's reply: "Which is *easier* to say, 'Your sins are forgiven,' or to say, 'Get up and walk?' But I want you to know that the Son of Man has authority on earth to forgive sins." So he said to the paralyzed man, "I tell you, get up, take your mat, and go home."

Jesus used a visible healing to confirm invisible forgiveness.

First Peter 2:24 says, "By his wounds we have been healed." According to Peter, the cross not only provides forgiveness but also healing. Have you embraced an "easier to say" tradition or a "harder to do" truth?

59

MINUTE 110

Cursed so We Could Be Blessed

What is the significance of the cross? Let's look at another blessing Jesus made available through Calvary. Galatians 3:13 says, "Christ redeemed us from the curse of the law by becoming a curse for us."

Some do not want to admit that curses exist because the idea sounds so primitive. But if they do not exist, why would Scripture inform us that Jesus died to redeem us from them? Sin is not only evil, but it is also cursed.

When we sin, we open our lives to sin's effects. Sin carries in itself the seeds of destruction. God never curses us, but our sins do. How do we break curses in our lives? Recognize the destructive patterns in our lives, turn to God, and renounce every belief and behavior that has opened the door to Satan. Proverbs 26:2 says an undeserved curse will not rest. A curse cannot rest on you if you learn to rest in the redeeming work of Jesus, on Calvary's cross.

MINUTE 111

Rejected so We Could Be Accepted

Before Jesus spoke His last time from the cross, He said, "It is finished." But what was finished? Mathew 27:46 reports that moments earlier, "About three in the afternoon, Jesus cried in a loud voice... 'My God, my God why have you forsaken me?'" Jesus was rejected, so we could be accepted.

Five verses later, the Bible records, "The curtain of the temple was torn from top to bottom." Josephus, an ancient historian, reported that the veil was four inches thick, was changed every year, and that horses tied to each side could not pull it apart. For thousands of years, God's presence resided primarily in a little room called the Most Holy Place that was shielded by this curtain. Only the high priest entered this room; this happened only once a year, while he was carrying atonement blood.

The veil was torn from the top, because God was indicating that the way into to His presence was not opened by the works of a mere man but by the work of heaven's Son. God never wanted to live in a little room but desires to live in the hearts of His people. The curtain has been torn, but it is up to us to choose to cross this threshold into His presence.

Section 3

LEADERSHIP

"The prerequisite of good leadership is not learning to control others, but first gaining control of oneself."

– DEREK GRIER

MINUTE 112
Leadership Myth #1

Twice a year, I travel to Ethiopia to train leaders for John Maxwell's EQUIP. I want to share with you some of the lessons. We are going to spend a few segments looking at the seven deadliest leadership myths.

Myth #1 is the idea that a person cannot lead unless he or she is on the top.[7] This is the misconception that leadership comes from simply having a position or title. Nothing could be farther from the truth!

In Exodus 18, we discover that Moses needed some guidance. It is surprising that God did not use a titled leader from within Israel to help Moses but his African father-in-law, Jethro. Exodus 18:24 says, "Moses listened to his father-in-law and did everything he said." No matter your title, if people respect you, you can positively influence them.

The true measure of leadership is influence—nothing more, nothing less. A person who has respect can influence others from any position.

MINUTE 113

Leadership Myth #2

The second most dangerous leadership myth is this notion: "When I get to the top, then I'll learn to lead."[8] Climbing into the cockpit of a jet airplane does not make you a pilot any more than having people call you "Pastor" will make you a good pastor. Becoming a good leader is a lifelong process. There is nothing automatic about it. Good leadership is learned in the trenches.

If you do not develop your leadership skills when the stakes are small and the risks are low, you are likely to get into major trouble if you have to learn after you are placed in high-level leadership. When the opportunity to lead comes, it is too late to prepare!

I want you to think about who God selected to replace Moses after his death. It was Joshua, the man the Bible calls "Moses' aid." Joshua served approximately forty years under the leadership of Moses before God released him into his own. It took forty years of training before Joshua was ready to lead. So be careful about trying to lead before you are ready.

MINUTE 114
Leadership Myth #3

The third myth we want to look at is what John Maxwell calls, "The Influence Myth." He said, "If I were at the top, then people would follow me."[9] Someone may give you a leadership title or position, but this will not make you a genuine leader. A position does not make a leader; the leader makes the position.

In Second Chronicles 10:6–19, Solomon's son Rehoboam became king, but it almost immediately fell apart. He decided to ignore the advice of his father's long-time counselors and listened to the advice of Pookie and Ray-Ray because they were his childhood friends. Just because you have known someone a long time, does not mean the person knows what he or she is talking about.

As a result of Rehoboam's foolish approach, the nation was irreparably split. Ten tribes revolted, and only Judah and Benjamin remained under his authority. It is far easier to lead in your imagination than in real life. Having the chief seat does not make a person a good leader. An organization will always grow or shrink to match the competence level of the person in charge.

MINUTE 115

Leadership Myth #4

Have you ever said to yourself, "If I were in charge, things sure would be different around here?" Listen to what King David's son, Absalom, said in Second Samuel 15:4 to anyone who would listen. "If only I were appointed judge in the land! Then everyone who has a complaint or case could come to me and I would see that they receive justice." The idea was that if he was on top, he would be more in control.[10]

There is nothing wrong in having a desire to improve your organization. But those without experience in leading will almost certainly overestimate the amount of control the person has at the top. The higher you go, the more you discover that many factors control an organization. Your position never gives you total control.

The Bible says that Absalom eventually seized the kingdom from his father but things quickly fell apart. It can sometimes be easier to criticize something than to improve it.

MINUTE 116

Leadership Myth #5

Today, we are going to look at the fifth myth people entertain. "When I get to the top, I'll no longer be limited."[11] Many people think that leadership is a ticket to freedom. Have you had thoughts like these from time to time?

- "When I get to the top, I'll have it made."
- "When I finally climb the organizational ladder, I'll have time to rest."
- "When I control the organization, I'll be able to do whatever I want."

These ideas are pure fantasy. On the contrary, when you move up in an organization, the weight of responsibility only increases. Usually, the more you move up the ladder in an organization, the responsibility you take on increases much faster than the amount of authority you receive. The higher you go, the more is expected of you and there is less room for error.

Jesus summed it up best by saying, "If anyone would be first, he must be servant of all." (Mark 9:35, ESV) The higher up you go, the more service is required and the less freedom you have.

MINUTE 117

Leadership Myth #6

The sixth deadliest leadership myth is this: "I can't reach my potential if I'm not the top leader."[12] People should strive for the top of their effectiveness, not to be at the top of the organization. Each of us should work to reach our potential but not necessarily the CEO's chair.

Sometimes, you can make the greatest impact from somewhere other than the first seat. Joseph was such an example. He was sold into slavery to an Egyptian official. In spite of his low position, his faithful leadership always resulted in promotion. Genesis 39:6 & 22 says, "Potiphar left everything he had in Joseph's care ... he did not concern himself with anything except the food he ate." Next, Joseph was unfairly sent to prison. In spite of his incarceration, Scripture records that "the warden put Joseph in charge of all those held in the prison, and he was made responsible for all that was done there." All of this was preparation for his final #2 position. He became the senior aide to Pharaoh.

Joseph never held the top seat, but God used him to save his entire region and family from certain disaster. Joseph became one of the most relevant biblical leaders of his era not because he was in the top seat but because he served well in the #2 chair.

MINUTE 118
Leadership Myth #7

We are going to look at the final leadership myth: The All-or-Nothing Myth. "If I can't get to the top, then I won't try to lead at all."[13] It is the mentality that says since I am not calling all the shots on the playground, I am going to take all my toys and go home. Because many people define success as being "on top," this is exactly what they do.

When individuals like this do not get the position they want, they become bitter, cynical, and often a hindrance to those who are in top levels of leadership. Paul says in Second Corinthians 10:13, "We will not boast beyond proper limits, but will confine our boasting to the sphere of service God himself has assigned to us." In other words, Paul found out what God has assigned him to do and became content with that.

A mentor once told a proud mentee, "You may think that you are the sharpest knife in the drawer, but you are not. You should celebrate the fact that you are in the drawer at all." We must focus on fulfilling our own potential, versus competing with someone else's.

MINUTE 119

Bob

This one EQUIP lesson leapt off the page for me, and I want to enlarge upon it and share it with you. The heading was this: "When Bob Has a Problem with Everyone, Bob Is Usually the Problem."[14]

How Do You Recognize a "Bob"?

1. Bob is a problem *carrier*. Like a contagious disease, people like Bob carry a "virus" that magnetically attracts negative situations.
2. Bob is a problem *finder*. It takes talent to fix problems, not to find them. Bob has eyes to see problems everywhere.
3. Bob is a problem *creator*. Bob seems to generate problems wherever he goes.
4. Bob is a problem *receiver*. Other people seem to know that Bob is a safe place to gossip, complain, and insult others. Remember that flies are attracted to stink.

My apologies to everyone named Bob, but begin to spot the Bobs in your life or organization, and make sure that Bob isn't you.

MINUTE 120
Leadership Pyramid

An essential part of being a good leader is knowing which rights to give up and which ones to fight for. In First Corinthians 9:3–5 & 12, Paul says, "This is my defense to those who sit on judgment on me." If you are going to be a leader, you have to get used to people judging you. He continues. "Don't we who are on missionary assignments for God have a right to decent accommodations, and a right to receive support for us and our families? (MSG) But we did not use these rights. Instead we put up with anything rather than hinder the gospel of Christ." Paul rightfully received compensation from other churches, but he knew that if he received it from this church, it would have created a problem.

The greater our calling, the more rights we will at times need to forfeit. Ministry is never a pyramid with its leaders on the top. True leaders see themselves at the bottom holding others up. Find a solid church and get on the bottom, so you can be on top!

Notes

SECTION 1
PERSONAL GROWTH

1. http://www.entheos.com/quotes/by_topic/Ralph
   +waldo+emerson.
2. http://lyricsfreak.com/k/knny+rogers/the+gambler
   .20077886.html.
3. *Equip* Volume 1, Notebook 6: "An In-Depth
   Journey into Transformational Leadership,"
   Lesson 3: The Leader's Time: Tick, Tock,
   Manage the Clock. P. 14, 2004.
4. Maxwell, John. *Today Matters: 12 Daily Practices
   to Guarantee Tomorrow's Success.*
5. http://thinkexist.com/quotation/if-you-can-
   control-a-man-s-thinking-you-don-t/821594.html.

SECTION 2
RELATIONSHIPS

6. The Spurgeon Archive: "Pray without Ceasing,"
   March 10, 1872. http:www.spurgeon.org/
   sermons/1039.htm.

Section 3
Leadership

7. Volume 2, Notebook 3: "360 Degree Leader," Lesson 1: The Myths of Leading from the Middle of an Organization. P. 2, 2004.

8. Volume 2 Notebook 3: "360 Degree Leader," Lesson 1: The Myths of Leading from the Middle of an Organization. P. 3, 2004.

9. Volume 2, Notebook 3: "360 Degree Leader," Lesson 1: The Myths of Leading from the Middle of an Organization. P. 3. 2004.

10. Volume 2, Notebook 3: "360 Degree Leader," Lesson 1: The Myths of Leading from the Middle of an Organization. P. 4, 2004.

11. Volume 2, Notebook 3: "360 Degree Leader," Lesson 1: The Myths of Leading from the Middle of an Organization. P. 5, 2004.

12. Volume 2, Notebook 3: "360 Degree Leader," Lesson 1: The Myths of Leading from the Middle of an Organization. P. 6, 2004.

13. Volume 2, Notebook 3: "360 Degree Leader," Lesson 1: The Myths of Leading from the Middle of an Organization. P. 6, 2004.

14. Volume 2, Notebook 2: "Winning with People," Lesson 4: Can We Build Mutual Trust? Pp. 18–19, 2004.

About the Author

Derek Grier currently serves as the founding pastor of Grace Church in Dumfries, Virginia. Grace Church began in 1998 with twelve people and has grown to more than three thousand members and over fifty life-changing ministries. In 2008, he founded the Dumfries Youth Center as an extension of Grace Church. It has served hundreds of high-risk children in the Dumfries area.

Dr. Grier studied business administration at Howard University. He earned a master's of education degree from Regent University and a doctorate in practical ministry from Wagner Leadership Institute. Dr. Grier serves on several boards and is an internationally certified associate trainer for Equip, which was founded by John Maxwell.

Dr. Grier was ordained a bishop in 2008 by Dr. Myles Munroe. He currently mentors hundreds of Christian leaders and business owners through the Renaissance Leadership Network. He has received numerous awards and is President of Virginia Bible College (VBC). VBC has established a partnership with Atlanta, Georgia-based Beulah Heights University and offers fully-accredited undergraduate, graduate and post-graduate degrees in business, leadership and theology.

Dr. Grier is also Senior Editor for bothsidesmag.com, which provides spiritual perspectives on hot-button issues of the day. He has been invited to the White House on several occasions and has been sought out by political leaders from both sides of the aisle. Dr. Grier has become a prominent voice in the Washington, DC, metropolitan area through his *Ministry Minute* and *Grace for Today* TV, radio, and Internet broadcasts, which have expanded both nationally and internationally.

Dr. Grier and his wife, Yeromitou, reside in northern Virginia and have two sons: Derek Jr. and David.

Other books by Dr. Grier: *60 Minutes of Wisdom: Insight in an Instant*

Next Steps

To continue your journey towards a more enriched, fulfilling and productive life with God, visit www.ahigherplan.com.

To Contact the Author

Follow Dr. Grier on social media.

 Facebook: www.Facebook.com/GraceChurchVA

 Twitter: www.Twitter.com/GraceChurchVA

 YouTube: www.Youtube.com/GraceChurchvaTV

You can also stream live on Sundays and Wednesdays at www.Lifestream.tv/gracechurch.

For more information, visit our websites at www.DerekGrier.com or www.GraceChurchVA.org.

Also Available from Derek Grier

From the voice that pioneered the inspiring *Ministry Minute* radio broadcasts comes *60 Minutes of Wisdom: Insight in an Instant,* a compilation of witty stories, lessons, and narratives by Dr. Derek Grier, that have improved the lives and captured the attention of hundreds of thousands of people in the DC metropolitan area.

Sixty insights, which could easily be compiled into over five hundred pages, have been boiled down into an easily accessible, down-to-earth format that provides time-tested, practical principles that give each reader the power to improve relationships, gain personal fulfillment, and elevate daily life. Each vignette requires only a minute to read but offers a lifetime of benefit.